TONE ŠKRJANEC
SKIN

TRANSLATED BY MATTHEW ROHRER & ANA PEPELNIK

TAVERN BOOKS

PORTLAND

Printed in the United States of America.

Cover art: Justin DePue, *Buddy Bolden,* 2001. Woodblock print.
Copyright © Justin DePue. Courtesy of the artist.

Author photo: DK.

Škrjanec, Tone, 1953-

ISBN-13: 978-1-935635-34-5 (paperback)
ISBN-13: 978-1-935635-35-2 (hardcover)

LCCN: 2014930897

FIRST EDITION

98765432 First Printing

TAVERN BOOKS
Union Station
800 NW 6th Avenue #255
Portland, Oregon
97209

www.tavernbooks.com

CONTENTS

THE SMELL OF THE SKIN

JAZZ

SKIN

THE SMELL OF THE SKIN

ON TRANSIENCY

i feel pain, suffering, death.
a room full of soft, warm bodies.
naked they giggle, rummaging caviar with their fingers
watching snow-capped mountain peaks
glittering in the sun as they slowly pass by.
i sit by the window, waiting for snow. it doesn't come.
but an evening does, in the early afternoon.
the lake still and motionless like pudding.
a few black tiny ducks with white beaks.
everything is somehow silver, made of light, cool weight,
and fast. it's a few minutes past midnight.
every passer-by touches me.

DEPENDING ON CLOUDS

suddenly i feel i need more space.
nothing but forests all around, for some moments they're dark blue,
then bright green. everything depends on clouds,
moving back and forth over the sky like big, gray lakes.
i'm not sure what i'm thinking about as i soak my feet
in a lukewarm lake, seemingly absorbed in thoughts,
and a white hairy dog trips by like a cumulus.
a little green bug lands on my elbow
for a moment, to take a breath.

HISTORY

rain was falling at night. i liked it, this darkness
and hollow chatting of space. then i fell asleep.
and dreamed, probably. i woke up
with some unknown taste in my mouth. maybe
common everyday life was happening to me,
only following different sequences,
with faces, bodies and voices that vanished inside me
a long time ago. like that pineapple yesterday.
how good it smelled and cried. and the cut piece of salami
persistently drying on a plate is also
part of history, as is the fly buzzing over it.

EVERYDAY LIFE

i'm looking at all that's living behind my eyes.
something black like a black bird on white skin.
milk is firm like a house. it forms
the hilliness of social landscape. lips
that leave a colorful trace on the edge of a coffee cup.
sleeping warriors in train stations,
burgers and pieces of fried chicken.

UNDULATION OF SKIN

undulations of the upper layers of skin
depend on hidden explosions inside,
when the world, like some big bloody jaw
shaped like a cracked tomato, descends upon it,
upon this supple, soft and warm flesh.
drab trousers against the skin, then all this
warm body tightening,
white shoes, transparent frames,
breasts weaved into a chewed up snake. very tiny
cuts from life. old poems and lukewarm beer.
through these glasses i don't see well and everything's crooked,
but i see anyway. what i see through the window is completely black.
there's no one making sure we're being calm.
actually, it's all about that. dim lights
of illuminated windows. undefined
though entirely familiar touches. we're all very serious
and reliable when playing. all the rest is a bad
idea, like italian evergreens. each foot
has its own ending and name. this one is called
andjelina. shaven and smooth like a leaf.

MORNING WASN'T PART OF THE PLAN

light, open windows and drizzle
in my head in the morning. the memory
of the evening is shattered like dreams.
it was twilight thick like a shadow,
all the lights off, only silent sounds
and lithe light from the TV
on naked bodies.
the scent of coffee latte in a big bowl,
hotel keys on a table
between tobacco fragments.
foreign, no man's land.
today we're going up a hill
that's also why we're nibbling on cookies.
as i bring them to my mouth
my hand still smells smooth,
of a stranger's skin. blind memories
of warm skin, moments of hesitation,
of whispering, driving through the night
and of a soft body wrapped in a towel
still live inside it.
i'm not talking about dreams,
i'm telling some old story
about a locomotive, lips

and convex hips.
i don't speak of dreams.
i'm bringing pieces of red
and orange oranges to my mouth.

FOXES

quite tranquil, we lit the cigarette very slowly
and then each of us,
each with our own eye,
carefully touched the horizon.
there were mountain brinks,
rocks and snow, probably chamois
and big piles of silence.
we slurped sour milk
cold biting our feet,
there was keith jarrett, too
and sounds of his piano
were like infinity
dripping into infinity.
our hands were too small
and the world too big to take it
with us around the lake.
some unknown butter cakes
on the horizon. everything very faint,
as if vanishing in the sky.
today we're going to pile up boards
however we want
out of pure love and completely without order
just to see how long

they'll stay in a pile.
and then those foxes
with shiny eyes may come.

A HOLE IN THE SKY

we have to write, because that which comes today
holds true for tomorrow. soft simmering of speech
intermingles with the rattling of an old tractor
into ambient morning music. birds
hiding in gigantic green tree tops
around our yard fall silent
just for a second and listen.
girls are rubbing fragrant oils and creams
into their naked and mostly tanned
bodies, until the very last hair, until the thin
slice, descending arrow-shaped
into the pubic area,
so the tight curves of their little bodies
(which our eyes follow automatically,
like simple machines) glitter like
frosted beer bottles from TV
commercials. because there's a hole in the sky. i watch
an island between my bent legs.
it's small, barren, and completely uninhabited.
once we went there for a visit by boat.
we treaded so carefully over the sharp rocks
and picked a bunch of wild garlic.

CROWS AND SEAGULLS

yesterday the day was cool and the evening even cooler.
a northern wind was blowing somewhere from the north. a young
    woman
with a strong lower jaw wearing a pink plastic flower
in her hair slowly sips her beer. i don't like her too much.
we talk about grapes, figs, about how they were still green and
    hard three days ago,
about nature which takes and gives, and about crows,
this year there are almost as many as seagulls.
the wonderful bush, full of pink blossoms
to which my gaze so often escapes, goes unmentioned.

EVENING BEFORE NIGHT AND NIGHT BEFORE MORNING

everything very weird. this gray-haired rock. stone with dark-gray
    skin
of a wrinkled dog. totally tame and mellow. green tea with a touch of
wild mint is quite bitter. a bird singing all night. we know
which one it was. we know it. the world i'm placing under my
    thoughts is like that.
nothing lasts forever. everything is very weird. bodies are beautiful.
they're climbing a hill and panting. when the first drops of rain
    start to drizzle
i grasp at their arm and squeeze under an umbrella. how
horrendously beautiful the warmth is, traversing between them.
    half of the sky covered with
thin clouds, beautiful faces aren't necessarily dark and young. trees
    aren't necessarily olive trees.
at night, when i'm sleeping, the past catches me helpless.
i dream of shiny, smooth lips and small, flat breasts
like a wave on a calm sea. ancient sensations. i escape
into early morning. sitting under a canopy, i can feel a scent of
    young trees
in the air. rain is slowly subsiding. drops sliding down greasy,
    spear-shaped
leaves of oleander. birds are reporting from all sides.
the body isn't listening to the head, it stubbornly rocks around

the world
leaving sticky drops behind. i cough, light a cigarette,
take a sip of cold tea. gray sky is stretching above me.
birds are singing from all sides. everything else is asleep.

BASIC THOUGHTS ON BEING

streets are shining.
the sun is falling straight,
directly on the treetops,
the day looking even
gentler than in the morning.
very slowly i sit around
in this moment of silence.
fall is coming.
september.
puddles on the street.
children in school.
again a lot of shut windows.
completely different silence in the morning.

PILING UP DICE

totally satisfied,
like that, in my pajamas in the evening,
completely naked actually,
skin relatively soft
on the rough textile
of the aged armchair.
a little bored and
chunks of lethargy.
i'm playing thinking.
a pile of differently shaped dice
most of them shapeless ideas,
also two dogs and one tabby cat.
maybe it's quite the opposite.
i'm piling them up into the shape of a moon.

NOISES ARE IN THE AIR

everything's temporary
in the shade of some unknown tree
standing by the shade of a flowering oleander
with pale pink blossoms.
some flowers, yellow and red,
open only in the evening
when actual shadows appear,
when the sun isn't so strong anymore,
when people and stories gradually
begin to disappear in the dusk. yet,
how some faces
appear just once
and never disappear again.

PRAGUE EARLY IN THE AFTERNOON

met a lip which reminded me
of a train from my youth. I slowly pull off
her panties, lift up her skirt to see
whether my hands still recognize
her warm hips. then it's confused morning
and still Prague in the Czech Republic.
it's quiet. I listen to the pulsing of the body. in mid-afternoon I sit
in a completely empty bar on a side street. I'm drinking beer.
dark leather, velvet and reddish dusk, lined with awful music.
the waitress brings a drink and a glimpse
of her left breast. time flies slowly. on a red wall
a big black and white photo of Marilyn Monroe in a white skirt.
a woman enters, focused and firm like an apricot,
like a small, tight pussy. then it's the road again,
slowly ascending and increasingly pulsing. I wish
you would sometime put on that kind haziness of yours,
which reminds me of a morning in Greece with a long walk on
      the slope
to the first coffee and goat yogurt. I love little events.
this can be a poem of today and this poem can be
for everyone separately, for birds and for stones.

TONGUE

the room is full of small staircases.
the soul smells of sweat
and has small, sharpened breasts.
I sit somewhat in the middle of the world
smelling fried anchovies.
I'm hungry. the eye slowly digests
a pile of round and tight tummies,
glittering in the twilight
like some mighty stars.
two naked legs are swinging
from a second floor window,
in the corner of the yard, two dogs
are synchronously talking to the sky.
I'm polishing memories. I'm soaking
my dried-up tongue deep
in something which might be the essence.
my eyes are closing
but I still feel
that I won't be able to sleep.
fiction is a tiny moment among reflections.

THE DAY THE RABBIT DISAPPEARED

the shaman raises his leg,
slowly lays it over his knee
takes off his shoe
and scratches his sole.
then, all enormous
in an antique, richly carved chair,
he rolls his thin goatee.
on the streets trembling from heat,
cold water is being sold
in plastic bags
and a few kinds of fruit i don't know.
resembling deer, girls
chattily walk
their bodies,
naked almost to body hair
and smelling like coffee.
today they kidnapped my rabbit
from the hotel room.
in the night, the wind blowing from the sea
smells of bananas.

MOSAIC: INFINITA TRISTEZA

this afternoon smells of elder
under which i parked my car.
yesterday afternoon, for example, smelled
of morocco, though just for a while.
because of this it's even harder for me to keep
my reason and objective judgment.
in the grass in the shade of a concrete fence
a black bird clumsily hops, my black neighbor.
his big bright eye
doesn't stop following me even for a moment.
his big shining eye.
he rubs his feathers, fixing himself
to be tall and beautiful among fresh
blades of grass.
the forest is squeezed between blocks of flats,
looking insignificantly small from here,
like a blueberry bush, and smaller
than the distance between eyes.
i remember some, dark brown
with a line, like candies used to be.
like ebony with a flaw.
or maybe they were black.
and it was night. black as lynx.
and pretty much infinitely sad.

SYCAMORES

the weather is in solid contrast
with body rhythm. i drive
through gray and damp air into
a tunnel of dense green trees.
these trees resemble sycamores.
two freckled brown pigeons
cross my path.
yesterday was saturday
so today must be sunday,
june 12, 2005, a day for classic
family lunches with at least three plates.
today, a tit bird flew
into our flat through
the wide open window.
it was a quick visit,
nervous little feathery head
turning around,
then back outside again into the green and blue,
everything like a happy end of a movie
where everybody smiles
and title credits run across them.
i watch white polished nails
how at first they touch and
then sink into gentle

pink flesh. fingers becoming
increasingly smooth, with little drops of silver
oozing over them.

TREES

sometimes i demand the maximum,
i expect everything to go over the edge,
that the tree at the end of the street
bloom red, like it normally does,
that the cherry tree behind the house, all weak
and crooked, put on white blossoms
again after two years.

FLESH OF SPIRIT

doors with a garden remained closed,
the lock half locked,
the bolt bolted, the stuffy cold
is like a foggy screen. knees cramped.
big temporary smiles
amid wet snow fields.
they're gray and two dimensional.
self-sufficient and beautiful, in a way.
each in its own way. houses are high
and gray. they're also brown but in a gray way.
the car is full of intoxicating weed stench.
white branches of brown and wet trees.
there aren't many people, some old german shepherd
deciding real slow in which direction
he will be carried away. i forgot something.
i've lost many things. it's warm
and machines are droning differently than the wall clock.
i adore empty cities
and juicy and round asses
that slowly and deliberately,
very pigeon-like, sway
along a narrow footpath that follows the green river like a ghost.

CREATURES

it's like that if you're alive.
little things everywhere.
the zoo and the racetrack.
breathing. flies
that crash
into the lit bulb.
some ancient instinct
entangles me into the woolen cardigan,
raising my gaze into the sky
which gray-curves over the oleander.
i'm listening as the wind
that i barely feel
makes the sea sound
like a big, old
noisy cafe.

BIRDS

traces of drops in the morning
in the dark puddle between the garage
and the muddy meadow.
a gray curtain, hung through the air.
black patches of snow
laying around
like some worm-eaten carcass.
a weird nervousness in the air,
maybe only in the body,
maybe only in the fingertips
searching for the first cigarette.
little birds with red
feathers on their wings,
i forgot their name again,
carefully glancing toward me
as i stand behind the window
rubbing my eyes.

STRENGTH

some strange and enormous strength is hidden inside me.
it's strange and enormous. it's hidden inside me.
it doesn't care about its weakness. it has a pussy
you can only dream of, when you lick your fingers. and vice versa.
positioning it on my leather two-seater from different angles.
it shaves the body regularly and systematically,
making it smooth like pudding. covering itself with a soft,
red blanket and sleeping long. dreaming.
i let it. without touching.

MEANING OF FOOD

who knows what negotiations will bring.
some snow or thin, transparent
ice which will cover everything that exists. maybe
even warm, incomprehensible tongues
licking it away to the skin. food is
extremely important, it prevents headaches,
oils the body properly so it doesn't rattle
while strolling slowly down the tree lane by the river.
we get along better this way,
constantly touching each other coincidentally,
sipping extreme amounts of teas and beers.
we're sitting close to each other.
smelling each other.

MIRACLES

black crows on the gray background
of a september sky.
miracles happen only occasionally.
just to discreetly
remind us of themselves.
a cloud which suddenly
breaks. music that touches the tip
of genitalia
very lightly with a tongue. the night,
when entirely dark
and entirely silent,
is never entirely silent.

ALL

all these black voices.
these crooked tree trunks
seem dead.
dark-silver bodies.
cracked sun.
brown river, slow
and smooth like the body.
trees with vivid blossoms
and women of different colors
and shapes. cool beer
in thick shade.
all
that is difficult
to grasp with words.

MOVEMENTS

this colorful and shapeless skirt
expresses mostly slenderness
and the elegance of moves. its
movement makes the pagan body rhythm
obvious. the body is a compact and
living shape like a rock, a mountain covered with moss.
giving it touch and soft curve
on the corners. it has everything. knowing art by heart.
a small pack of rhythms burnt on the skin.
warm breath. sweaty sticky skin.
symbolic and actual meaning
moving from the shade of one tree
into the shade of another.

TIME THEFT

the picture i've kept in my mind to this day,
wrapped in a woolen scarf, winter jacket zipped to the neck,
uptight and kind of self-sunken,
that position, the entire composition
which i keep in my mind—
leaning on the elbow, left leg slightly bent
at the knee, to ensure the most comfortable
and absolutely the most attractive position
of a naked body, is a fact. it exists in memory.
some completely coincidental dog,
tousle-haired mix
of mixtures of unknown breeds
that for some seemingly
pointless reason races by
for a second, for a long moment,
covers the glorious dual parade
because of the unfortunate terrain configuration. touching
of glances isn't a sin. nor is it touching.
a sin is a delicate matter and a time theft.
not my thing. it's winter outside, cold
and high piles of gray, dirty snow.

JAZZ

let there be jazz, i say to myself, let the song gargle from the speakers.
let it be sad, rambling and wordless.
heavy heads of white elder blossoms, leaning on an old brick fence.
forever trapped into a few short sentences
flying around me like flakes of snow.

JAZZ

DUST

there were some average dreams.
there were two long waves, which were,
they were of the type that were cutting the lake.
there was some night, it was completely silent,
actually everything was closed,
no problems,
everybody was healthy, no cancers,
no similar deadly troubles,
just the usual fucking, and none of the who loves who,
who stuck what and where into who,
it was truly beautiful, it was a long smooth lake,
tiny colorful lights everywhere,
there were two grayish pigeons, a bunch of ducks, they were black
with white beaks. and a flock of tomtits on our balcony,
five to ten fluttering grams. my body aches.
I won't tell anything, I won't speak,
my peace is the silence of the guilty one, darkness outside,
it's cold, and who cares, I care,
it's not all the same to me, my muscles ache,
my body is telling me something,
some old story which everybody knows,
I know it too, or at least I have a hunch
on some slightly metaphysical level.

nothing is serious to me, my body is the one I rent,
I don't feel like being anything.
I feel awful, I sit in a car and I feel awful,
it's totally silent, perhaps that's why,
just the engine can be heard and the breathing.
to me a lot doesn't mean that much. to me a lot of self-admiring
    giants
are just some weak Arabic versions of a Saturday walk,
to me sometimes being small means a lot,
that I'm actually forever infinitely small,
it hurts me when my dearest ones think
I can handle electricity, all those trivial installations,
that sitting in silence and listening isn't a statement
and that I like to be lost in thoughts, go silent, that everyday
    vanities are inborn to me,
and I let them be just a funny obsession,
that dust on objects is a serious matter that doesn't forgive,
that the world is becoming a more simple-minded idea with every
    passing day,
and unfortunately not just the fact that everything happens by
    the way,
a little remark, a few camels, some totally tiny animals,
a barely sensible perception of something that was never quite for

real.
I'm the one that stood by some grave the other day
it was the same grave from years ago, when I was talking
nonsense somewhere inside of me:
look, look what is happening to me, but nothing did,
almost nothing special, just we were dying piece by piece.
we were standing there and the world wasn't waiting, it just was
there somewhere,
like some fucking eternity that knows everything, that understands
everything
but in fact it doesn't get it at all. it's cold outside and there's snow
and I wish I was happy but it somehow doesn't work,
something always comes in the way, it happens all the time, always
these structures,
even though we are always beautiful, we always have our naked
body
which glitters like a star.
always beautiful as a star.
and I don't want to go home.

GRAY LIGHT

this morning a pile of hollow dilemmas,
nervous hesitations. the day gray
and kind of impersonal. like it's not even there.
an elongated pink nude on the wall
is from yesterday, from yesterday's images.
fast speech runs over the music,
silent touching of a pianist's fingers
where shadows move away from the gray light.
there's absolutely no need.
nor was there any. circular saws are singing outside.
preparing bushes for the spring
which is getting ready to leap into the summer.
even the dog jumps up and down
the stairs, the speakers crackle,
membranes are conspiratorially pulsating,
a woman passes by the window, she doesn't hop,
she's giggling, speaking into the phone,
and her hair bounces.
a saw continues to play on its living and dead
nature. memories descend
in the evening like a flock of birds.
they play with colors which
the eyes just start to make up.

breasts touch the strings,
making them bend and
release an unclear, quiet sound.

RAHAT LOKUM

in the morning rain has risen.
birds in the water to their knees, sheltered by heavy treetops.
i'm hollowly sliding over asphalt in a car that's accompanied by
    trees
like a wall, like silent, dignified guards.
everything's pretty normal, things covered with vinyl
so that color doesn't fall off, so their character doesn't escape.
thoughts are coming from the air through lungs. i'm avoiding
    puddles
which remind me of little, cloudy and upset lakes.
behind glass windows striped with raindrops
are people in pink cardigans, muddling through the world
with bare, sweaty hands on the wheel. bringing gifts
sealed in cardboard boxes. something's moving inside them
with a pleasant, light smell and making sounds that aren't a song.
the song is someplace else and we can't hear it.
that's why we listen to what we have. and i don't mean
whining and moaning, nor snuffling verging on joy.
we're on a special road, bringing important messages
in the shape of little sweet cubes that respond only to the touch
    of a tongue,
but everything puzzles us—wind, hydroplaning, the blackbird's
    yellow beak

carelessly jumping around in the rain,
a blunt can opener, all the beauties of animate and inanimate
    nature
demanding our immense and absurd attention.

CARS

i don't care about all these expensive cars,
all these material goods,
as long as there's love,
says some old, half-evergreen song.
it talks much more specifically about chevrolets,
cadillacs and ford mustangs, long, black and shiny.
people loved to sing it,
they kept adding their own types of cars,
rings with diamonds, mansions on hills,
their most burning ambitions,
a color TV, because it's an old song.
who cares about all this, everybody agrees,
as long as there's love.
and we believe them.
i look with my eyes wide open
when i'm drunk.
my dreams are different.
they're quite shivery, restless and loud,
i don't remember their real faces,
but i can roughly summarize their message in a few sentences:
let it be revolution all the time and let it win.
i'm not afraid of any birds.
of any white socks.

i wander in the dark.
touching only with blunt fingers.

WINTER POEM ABOUT OTHER TIMES

I don't know how to put it,
I don't know. something is touching me,
but I don't know who it is.
that's why I'm always looking,
searching and when I see, then
I look some more. I'm watching
you quite coincidentally and by the way.
you're lying on the edge of my viewing angle,
sleeping peacefully and silently like a fish.
I'm once again and again
writing something, some words,
images and feelings, which are preparing
to escape, to sink forever
somewhere deep into me
and appear as blood only
when I get hurt, in the form of crystals
which flare up for a moment in the light
and disappear fast under the tongues of animals.
I don't know, I feel something
but I don't know what. is it the shuddering
of fear, joy or strength
when I make a small house with my hands.
is this then the freedom

of which they sometimes speak.
is this a soft house made of hands
more than just feelings.
a fish with wings,
a girl, kissing someone.
honestly. I don't know.

A POEM ABOUT A CHAMOIS

TO JANI SAX

at certain times you have to go silent.
leave pure silence, all to itself,
so pain can overcome pain.
today i don't stand all restless in a line of numb glances
that creak like footsteps on sharp white gravel
on a plain, snuggled between mountains,
in the suburb of a town of rust-colored houses.
today i sit here alone, i'm snuggling against the cold window,
keeping silent, looking through the window, observing the wind.
i'm watching it toy with leaves,
and i'm writing this short poem about a chamois.
its eye is wide open and blue like the velvet sky.
we're so close to each other, yet entirely apart.
today is a silent day. today the wound is open.

TOO MUCH VOID

too many words
is not enough words.
every stone has its own story.
every shadow a few good ideas about moving.
i feel empty, like only a town can be
or a room where you're not alone,
sitting in silence, and the tongue touching
dried lips can be heard, and the motions
are slow like the traveling of shadows. in the garden
a few people sitting around in the shade
of a tree, quietly as plants,
and high young grasses
of uncontrolled green origin.

A FEW WORDS ON TIME

what should we do nowadays,
when in a second
a computer sprinkles an infinity
of delicious corpses,
where should we drink wine
and lick each other's skin.
will we step, as we are now,
blind and deaf,
sworn lovers
of the rough sax breath,
on the same road again,
fill our lungs with fresh dust,
and search, to search and find nothing.
to establish a path as a path once more,
a wish as a wish, an eye as an eye,
ourselves as a shivery hairy animal
that camped out beneath the spruce.
everybody hurries while time remains totally calm,
as if it has stopped.
even music grows slowly,
like a tree.

TIME: MOMENT

it's true, approaches might be different,
but you can't demand just whatever you want from an actor.
then you'll get a lie, fluttery babbling,
some intermediate conditions. just words.
not naked but tired,
chewed over thousands of times
like the pussies of some women
i know. these coffeehouse debates
are not necessarily bad,
these dizzy skips from the general
to the specific. when night is high
the tongues are mating. i undress with my eyes.
my love drags her hand
under the table and gently
rubs my cock under the fabric of my jeans.
my girl kisses me shamelessly
deep in the mouth at mid morning
in a smoky cafe, when her tongue has
the intoxicating flavor of strong coffee
with a sprinkle of sugar. self-sufficient
like fresh snow on a bough. very confident.
both very much within. within the moment.
we're grasping it with our claws.

AUTUMN MORNING

the wet eye of a deer
a thick layer of velvet in the sky

FLAGS

the sun is stored behind the clouds.
a bit nervous.
my legs are itchy in several places.
i think i can see the end
in infinity,
that i can hear voices
from very far away,
calling and cursing.
sheets are flying in the wind,
not flags. the house is sleeping.
a gray tabby cat is napping in the doorway.

A PILE OF PAST TRACES ENTERING THE PRESENT

first i reach the glass with my eyes
only then with my left hand.
it's morning again and it's happy
in a slightly melancholic way.
black leaves of a red flower
on a barred window
grow to mid-thigh.
little blue symbols are scattered
completely randomly and very closely
on soft white fabric.
like watching a blossoming meadow from a distance.
there are marches and horsemen
with covered faces, then a stony dock
and a door, leading to nothing.
a large body from cool jade.
a herd of violet light is grazing on it.
sometimes a word too many, sometimes too few,
sometimes redundant and even so bothersome
that there's no need for it.
need is an incredibly greedy and wild animal
which attacks from different levels with outstanding determination.
sometimes it's made up
and drawn out like some boring novel

or TV news.
words can be redundant, even in the way.
the body has its own tongue
but body language
doesn't know words.
it doesn't have the slightest clue
about divine revelation.
nerves reside in my legs.
today they opened all the windows wide
and they're listening to hank williams yodeling.
they keep dancing a little,
moaning passionately
and stomping with their little feet,
which drives me nuts.
a poem is a black bird squatting
in thick tree shade in the summer singing something to itself.
a soul is a rapt horse at a railway station,
a hard round stone on the asphalt is a rabbit on the lookout.
skin is a manifestation of the soul.
green to the touch. standing on the verge of a clearing
with its big branched antlers
watching, breathing in and smelling damp moss
completely straight, almost motionless.

A POEM

poetry is a manifestation of absolute freedom.
everything i write is real and tingles when touched.
everything's got a name, it pulsates, smells nice and sniffs,
revealing its naked, slightly bent shoulders.
i forgot the rest, maybe i'll write it down some other time,
maybe i'll let it move around among us
forever and offer itself with touches,
as we sit by the open window, all frail,
in a small room, mixing something into our tobacco.

LONG POEM

in most cases things and events are related with tapes.
causes and consequences can be seen, exceptions seem
    coincidental
until they recur. a long poem does not write itself.
there are too many disruptive effects. music, speech
and everything that's carelessly thrown in.
i hate to talk to machines, although it happens.
i talk to myself. i make mistakes, i correct them and repeat them
    again.
if you press the right key something happens. you ring, for
    instance,
but nobody answers. the doors remain closed.
above, the sky is coughing. at the moment, trees are motionless like
    parked cars.
a woman in a bar is spinning around a silver metallic pole.
because it's evening, even the sky's somehow silvery and endless.
her name is condoleesa or katherine and she talks like silence.
i write by beginning with one, then i start to add and then i push
    in the words.
sometimes it goes fast, other times it lasts, and corrections of
    some steps
and figures are essential. on the issue of form and twists: i like
    seals more than snakes

but snakes are more colorful. plus: fresh pancakes with jam
on the top of mount triglav as a tribute to a friend and deer.
i almost feel like listing, stringing names,
rummaging through my life a little, looking back into history,
grating, stirring and kneading, telling some private story,
a game of coincidental sets of people and events,
that would project from the context like some clumsy, spasmodic
      dance that isn't tango
but a stormy undulation of the sea throwing you around
until you lose direction, and i don't think i'd like to walk
around those old streets in šiška again that change less than
      people.
i don't like to remember all the memories. i don't want to touch
      the things
that were again, but i do anyway. i wrote something,
everything else may keep wandering through the body and
      moping with my subconscious.
totally drunk with feelings. she doesn't undress in the real sense
      of the word.
sometimes a word has a hidden meaning. sometimes it lies like a
      mirror.
in some musical subcultures the hoarse, broken voice
and sharp bouzouki is a quality. only what comes from the heart,

not from the head. dance is a trance. walking on burning embers.
    here an opera doesn't count.
in fact she's not even undressing. she's already naked when she
    first appears.
i look through the window and immediately entangle myself with
    clouds.
i'll admit i don't know them. i speak from memory. i read things
    only from the papers
sometimes. i think about charles baudelaire's prose poems
and in the next moment about some old movie on turkish
    invasions from one of the republics
of an ex-yugoslavia. everyone wanted to have fun, a healthy
    meditation,
not the endless waiting for something which might not even
    happen.
her skin is smooth and tight. at first a big nothing and silence,
then small piles of various lights, noise from cars and overloud
    music.
i'm sitting by the sea, drilling a hole into a stone with a swiss army
    knife,
houses are shivering cubes without faces. black is white.
white is still white. women are shaved into a short vertical with
    sharp blades.

in no time we're uncompromisingly looted by the class enemy.
by abstract dictate of shapeless structures. pretty helpless.
bruised from all directions, the lacquer peeling off and signs of
    rust starting to show.
middlemen with time and words. her skin looks tender and kind,
it has a color of fresh copper.
in a town you have to climb a hill if you want a view of the world.
the horizon is house-eaten. a raft of stupid things sprinkled on paper
will be blown by the wind. kind certificates of diligence. occasionally
    i lick
my wounds in secret. at times i briefly and secretly touch somebody
though, with a pang of guilt, i have to admit
that i learned to hold back my tears and wrinkle my forehead wisely.
when i stepped off the airplane, hot and thick air burst into me
with force and hollow noise. people spoke an almost completely
    incomprehensible language.
they talked quickly, catching shades of houses and trees all the time.
as we drove by an old fort, kids played football on the meadow
in front of it, we drank cold water from plastic bags.
i'm looking at the fluttering parade of schoolgirls in ties and gray
    skirts
and a tall tree in the background, hung with pink grapes.
hotel windows were high above the ground and you couldn't open

them.
i was looking far into infinity. maybe facing home.
the room was filled with hollow silence, and a big black hole was
    gaping
where there was sea all through the day.

STUFFY

today things are placed differently,
atoms, crookedly assembled, aren't capable
of following the storyline or composing a reasonable sentence.
helplessly they reach out their little hands toward new dimensions
which they turn down arrogantly
in an almost humiliating way that we all know.
not throwing them even a pitiful glance
when they straighten their skirts or rush to powder their noses
    and stuff,
to the cold toilet covered with ceramic tiles
in which light reflects
the colors of rainbow. today things are placed differently.
clouds aren't even there, for example, especially
if we ignore that fluffy one
like a duckling there behind the horizon
stair-like defined by skyscrapers.
the air is evaporating, asphalt is burning, girls are cooling off
marilyn monroe style, lifting up their skirts,
waving them like flags at a national celebration.
they shave their hair everywhere, some even on their heads.
pollen that collects in eye corners,
mother superior of all deserts, is not relevant today.
trees have beautiful thick dark-green leaves

making thick shade. actually they don't make anything,
they're just there, letting thick shades fall on their own.
that's just the silent agreement of trees with the sun.
they're very magnificent and kind, like a home.
i'm writing a poem.
fingers first stick to the ballpoint,
then to the keyboard.
drops of sweat are gliding over my forehead.

WALKING

such a sticky day today.
coins clang in my pocket as i walk.
piles of ducklings are squatting in the shade of a tree
which could, at a quick glance, be a willow.
two women with legs bare to the knees are laughing
and gesticulating blessedly while crossing the street
that winds around the lake. walking is important.
thinking while walking. bodies while walking.
three cyclists on the top of the stairs are from another world.
covered with science-fiction helmets,
all red and flushed, looking like aliens.
while you walk you meet many almost divine creatures,
i.e. ducks, which i have already mentioned,
or this one here, sitting all by itself by the lake
and, seemingly without purpose, widely opening its beak,
so its long and slender neck is beautifully tightening.
such a sticky day, and yet
such a nice evening's silence,
just cars, birds, and oars
from afar hitting the lake,
and it seems that we animals are mostly satisfied.

LIFE ABOVE TOWN

the road slowly curves around the castle hill.
there's a castle on the hill.
a few bars are in the castle,
a souvenir shop,
some dark and damp
castle halls, they've been there forever,
are dim and stifling.
at the very top is a great view
of Ljubljana which is losing itself
in mist on the edges.
groups of walkers and tourists,
a few dogs, besides birds the only animals
pointlessly hopping around.
bushy treetops
with their thick green shades.
we're sitting on wooden benches.
unaccustomed to freedom,
we stare into the sky
like a deer tongue.
it's so fluttery today
though slightly bent in a postoperative way
and unusually silent.

HERON

i have a few clumsy words
a little perforated boat
and a sensual bird of undefined size
to communicate with the world.

ABOUT THE AUTHOR

Tone Škrjanec is a poet and translator who was born in Ljubljana, Slovenia, in 1953. After teaching for a short period, he worked as a journalist for nearly ten years. Since 1990, he has been a program coordinator at the Cultural Centre KUD France Prešeren in Ljubljana.

He has published eight books of poems, most recently *Noises are in the Air: selected and very old poems* (2012). His poems can be found in many contemporary anthologies of Slovenian poetry and have been translated into numerous languages. As an author, he likes to collaborate with musicians; some of these fusions of poetry have been recorded and are available in Slovenia.

In addition to being a writer, he is also a translator, mainly focusing on contemporary American literature, including works by William S. Burroughs, Charles Bukowski, Gary Snyder, Frank O'Hara, Timothy Liu, Paul Blackburn, Joseph Ceravolo, Jack Hirschman, Kenneth Koch, Jack Spicer, Anselm Hollo, and Kenneth Rexroth. He also translates from Croatian and Serbian. He lives and works in Ljubljana where he enjoys drinking green tea during the day and likes a pint of good beer in the evening.

ABOUT THE TRANSLATORS

Matthew Rohrer is the author of seven books of poems, most recently *Destroyer and Preserver* (2011). He has co-translated poems by Tomaž Šalamun (with the author), Virgil Banescu (with the author), and Volker Braun (with his mother).

Ana Pepelnik is a poet and translator who was born in Slovenia in 1979. She has translated many American poets into Slovene, including Elizabeth Bishop, James Schuyler, and Noelle Kocot.

TAVERN BOOKS

Tavern Books is a not-for-profit publisher of poetry. We publish books in translation from the world's finest poets, new works by innovative writers, and revive out-of-print classics. We keep our titles in print, honoring the cultural contract between publisher and author, as well as between publisher and public. Our catalog, known as The Living Library, sustains the visions of our authors, ensuring their voices are alive in the social and artistic discourse of our modern era.

THE LIVING LIBRARY

* forthcoming

Tavern Books is funded, in part, by the generosity of philanthropic organizations, public and private institutions, and individual donors. By supporting Tavern Books and its mission, you enable us to publish the most exciting poets from around the world. To learn more about underwriting Tavern Books titles, please contact us by e-mail: tavernbooks@gmail.com.

MAJOR FUNDING HAS BEEN PROVIDED BY

The Libra Foundation

TRUBAR FOUNDATION

This book was published with the support of Trubar Foundation at the Slovene Writers' Association, Ljubljana, Slovenia.

THE PUBLICATION OF THIS BOOK IS MADE POSSIBLE, IN PART, BY THE SUPPORT OF THE FOLLOWING INDIVIDUALS

Anonymous
Gabriel Boehmer
Dean & Karen Garyet
Bill Howe & Joy Bottinelli
Ana Jokkmokk
Mark Swartz & Jennifer Jones
Robert & Jan Jones
The Mancini Family

Dorianne Laux & Joseph Millar
Paulann Petersen & Ken Pallack
Roby Roberts & Lael Pinney
Pierre Rioux
Mary Ann Ryan
Marjorie Simon
Bill & Leah Stenson
Ron & Kathy Wrolstad

ACKNOWLEDGMENTS

Thank you to Michael McGriff, Tavern Books, and all who helped put this book together. And thank you to the editors of the following journals who helped bring Tone's poems to America: *Barrel House, Circumference, Explosion Proof, Le Zaporouge* (Denmark), *Salt Hill,* and *Washington Square.*

COLOPHON

This book was designed and typeset by Michael McGriff. The text is set in Garamond, an old-style serif typeface named for the punch-cutter Claude Garamond (c. 1480-1561). Arial Black is used for the displays. Arial Black, a contemporary sans serif font with broad industrial applications, was designed at Monotype by Robin Nicholas and Patricia Saunders. *Skin* appears in both paperback and cloth-covered editions. Printed on archival-quality paper by McNaughton & Gunn, Inc.